My Big & Easy Five-Finger Piano Book

Volume 1

arranged by Kevin Olson

Note from the Arranger

One of the best things about learning to play the piano is being able to play melodies that are familiar to you. This book is full of well-known songs, hymns, and carols, arranged for the beginning pianist in a variety of styles. There is a chart at the top of each piece illustrating where your hands will be placed. Once you feel comfortable with each song, try giving it a bigger sound by adding the accompaniment, played by a teacher or friend. I hope these arrangements add to your enjoyment of learning to play the piano. I wish you all the best as you continue developing your skills in music making—it is a gift that will keep on giving back to you and others throughout your life!

Best wishes,

Kevin Olson

Kevin Olson

Table of Contents

Note Guide

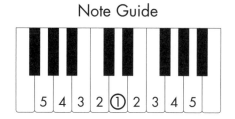

Bridge Over Troubled Water

Paul Simon

Slowly, in two (♩ = ca. 72)

mf When you're wea - ry, feel - in'

small, when tears are in your

eyes I will dry them___ all. I'm on your

Teacher Duet: Student plays one octave higher.

mp
with pedal

FJH2124

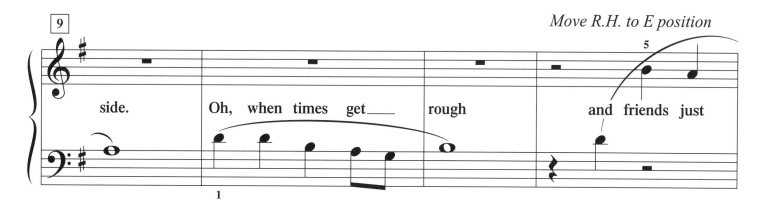

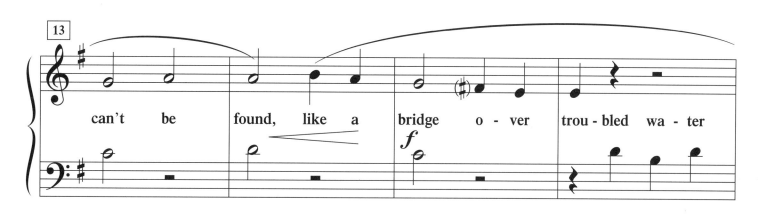

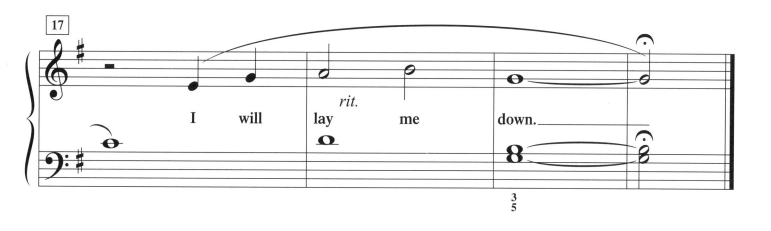

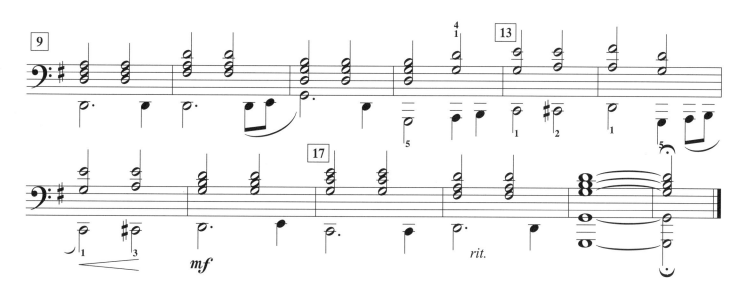

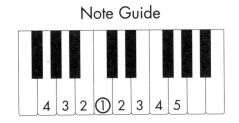

The Lion Sleeps Tonight

George David Weiss, Hugo Peretti,
Luigi Creatore, and Solomon Linda

Fast and swinging ($\downarrow$ = ca. 112)

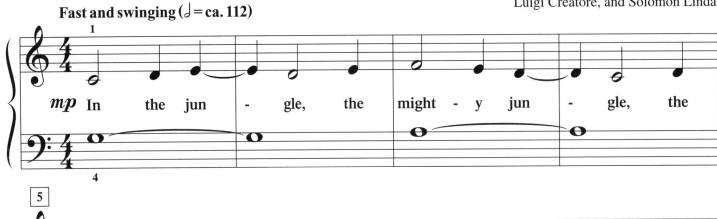

In the jun - gle, the might - y jun - gle, the

li - on sleeps to - night.

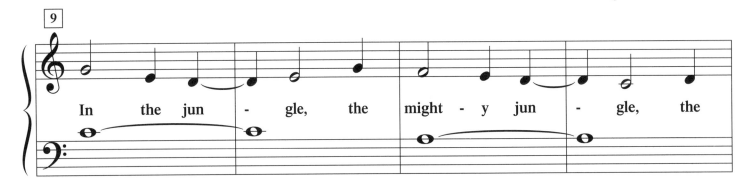

In the jun - gle, the might - y jun - gle, the

Teacher Duet: Student plays one octave higher.

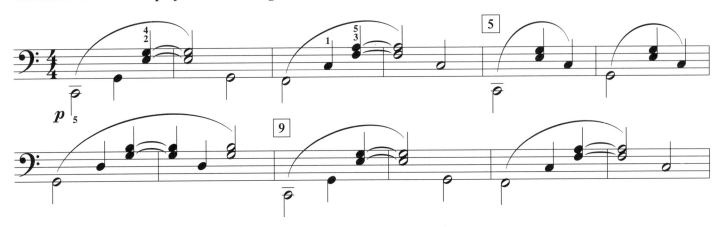

FJH212

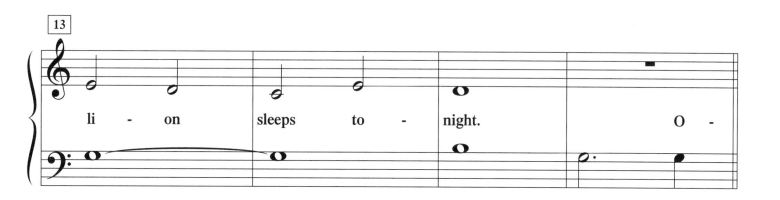

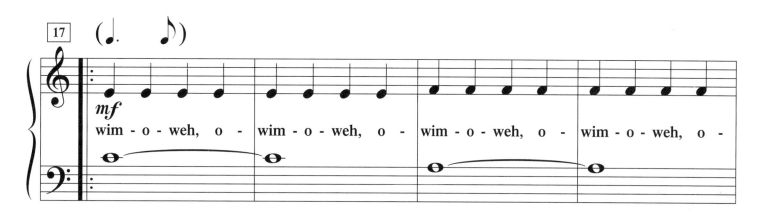

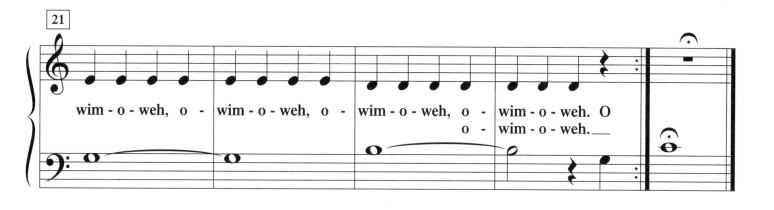

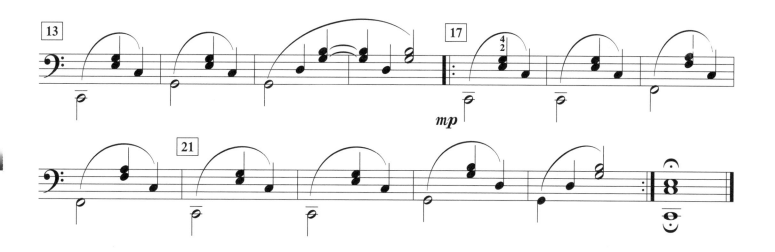

Note Guide

Rocky Top

Boudleaux Bryant and Felice Bryant

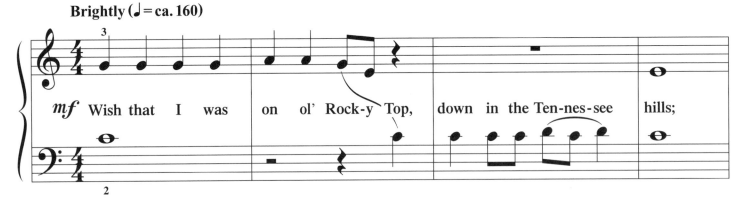

Brightly (♩ = ca. 160)

mf Wish that I was on ol' Rock-y Top, down in the Ten-nes-see hills;

Ain't no smog-gy smoke on Rock-y Top, ain't no tel-e-phone bills.

Once I had a girl on Rock-y Top, half bear, oth-er half cat;

Teacher Duet: Student plays one octave higher.

mp

FJH2121

Move both hands to F position

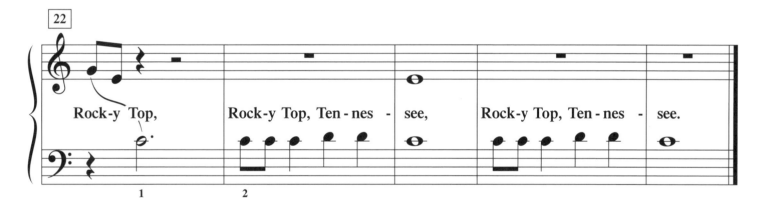

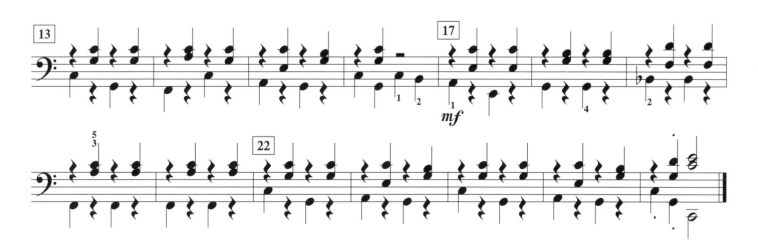

Note Guide

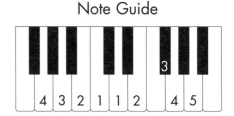

Where Is Love?

from the Columbia Pictures—Romulus Film *Oliver!*

Lionel Bart

Moderately (♩ = ca. 144)

Where _____ is love? _____
Where _____ is she _____

Does it fall from skies a - bove? _____
who I close my eyes to see?

Is it un - der - neath the wil - low tree that
Will I ev - er know the sweet hel - lo that's

Teacher Duet: Student plays one octave higher.

mp with pedal

FJH2124

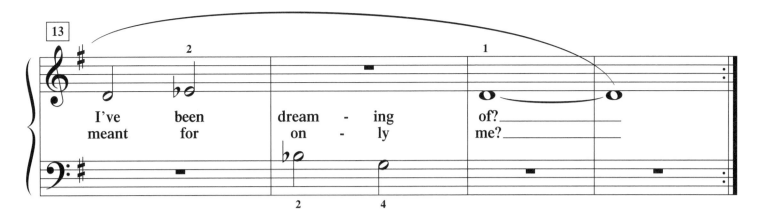

I've been   dream - ing   of?_____
meant   for   on - ly   me?_____

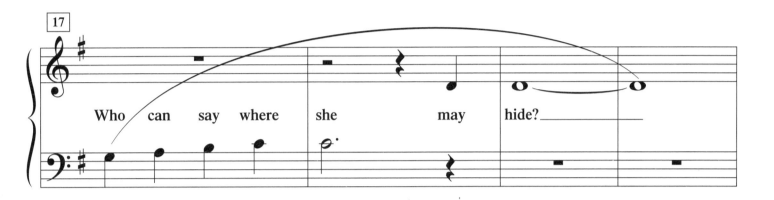

Who   can   say   where   she   may   hide?_____

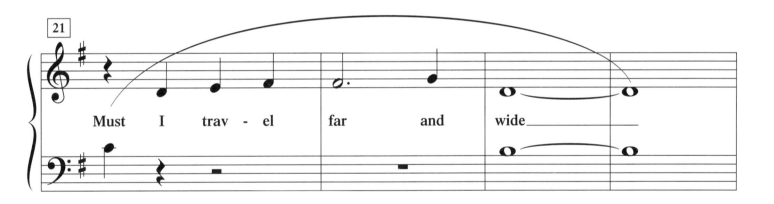

Must   I   trav - el   far   and   wide_____

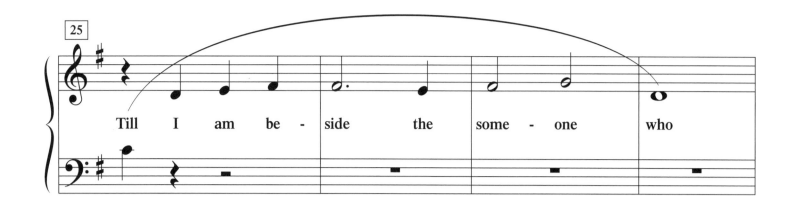

Till I am be - side the some - one who

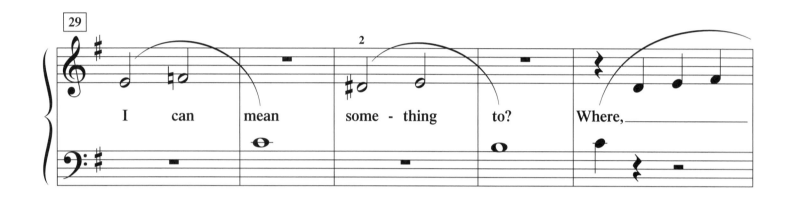

I can mean some - thing to? Where,_____

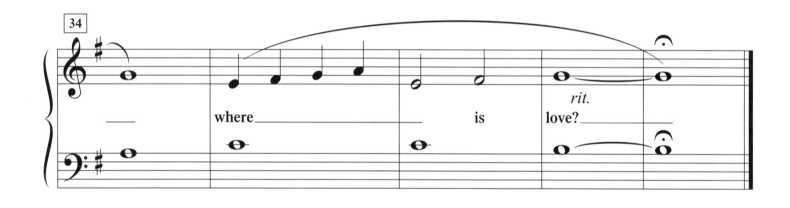

_____ where_____ is love?_____

rit.

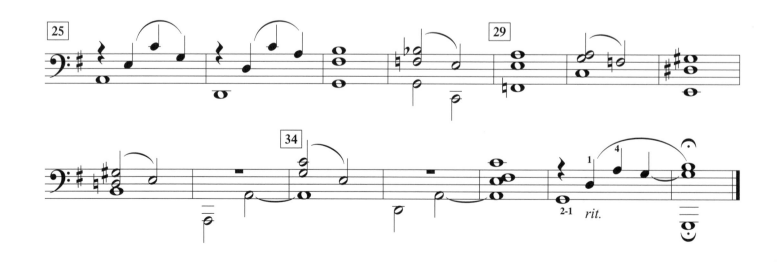

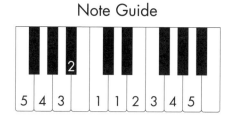

The Chicken Dance

Music and lyrics by Werner Thomas and Terry Rendall
English lyrics by Paul Parnes

Teacher Duet: Student plays one octave higher.

FJH2124

FJH2124

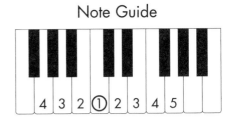

Ode to Joy

from *Symphony No. 9, Opus 125*

Ludwig van Beethoven

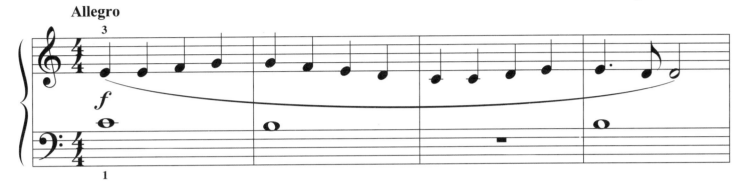

Teacher Duet: Student plays one octave higher.

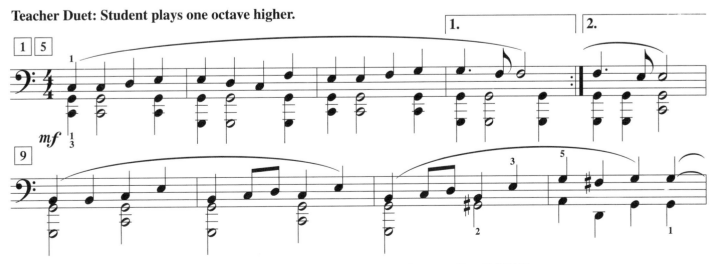

FJH2124

15

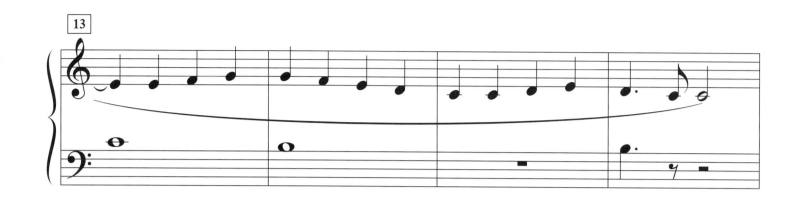

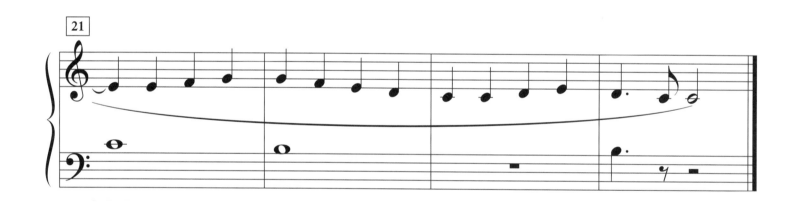

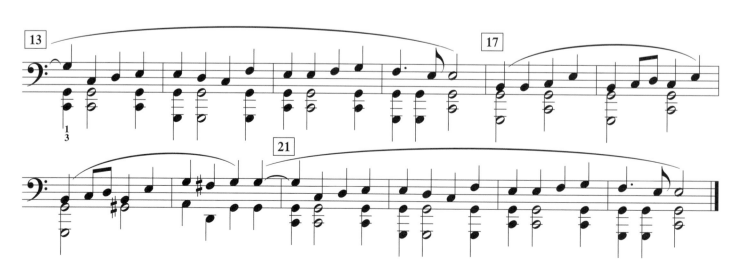

FJH2124

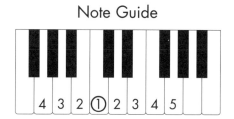

Hallelujah Chorus

from *The Messiah*

George Frideric Handel

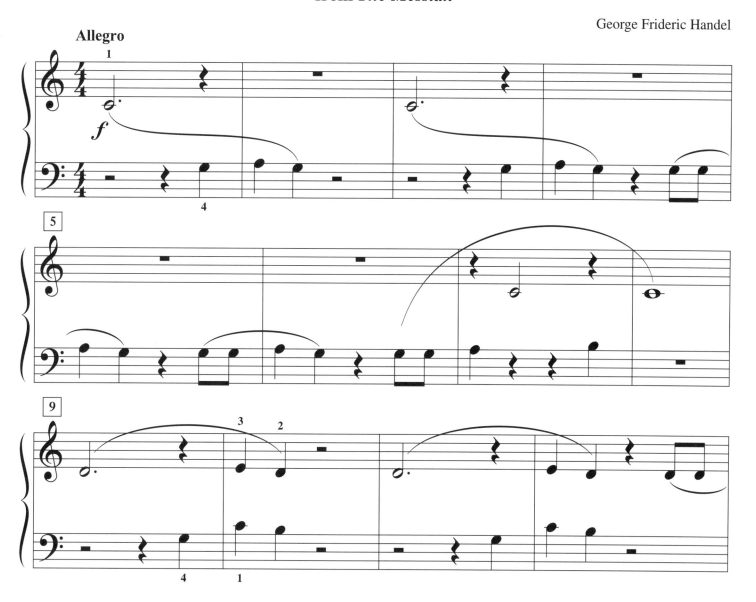

Teacher Duet: Student plays one octave higher.

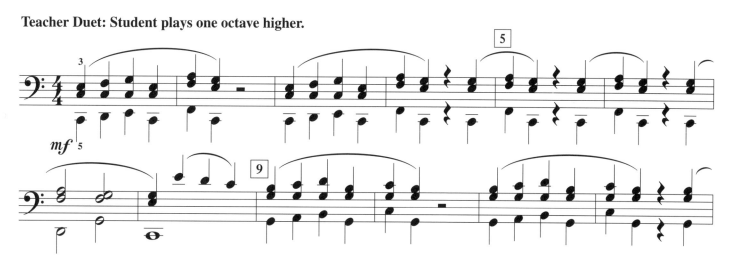

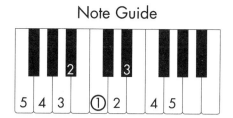

Note Guide

Ave Maria

Opus 52, No. 6

Franz Schubert

Moderately; expressively ($\quarternote$ = ca. 72)

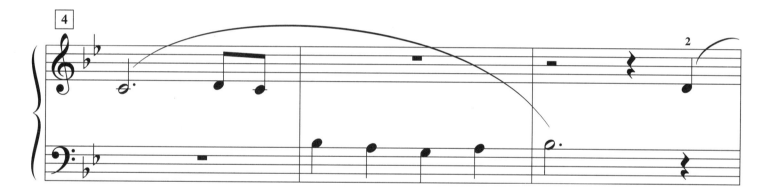

Teacher Duet: Student plays one octave higher.

FJH2124

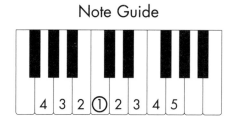

Note Guide

Eine Kleine Nachtmusik
(K. 525)

Wolfgang Amadeus Mozart

Teacher Duet: Student plays one octave higher.

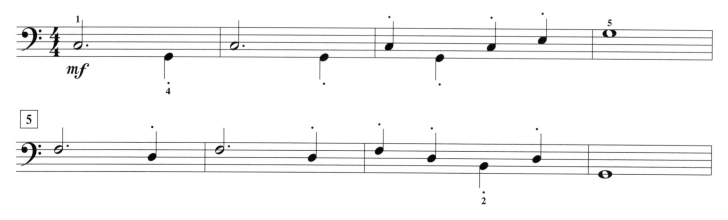

FJH2124

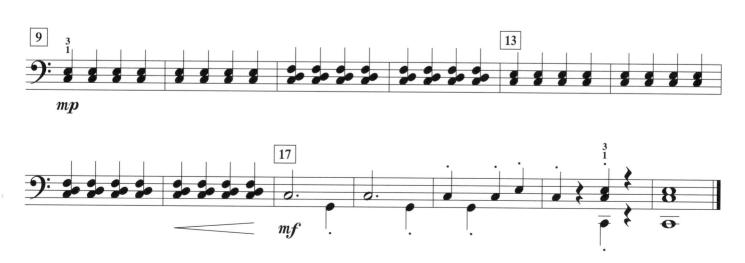

Note Guide

Jesu, Joy of Man's Desiring

Johann Sebastian Bach

Teacher Duet: Student plays one octave higher.

FJH2124

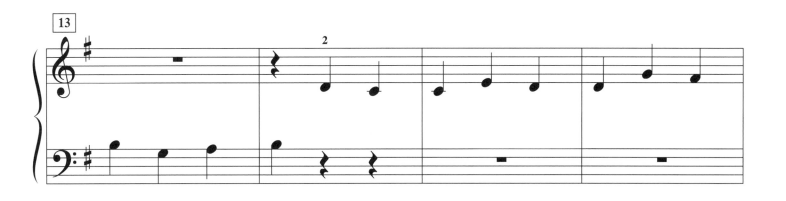

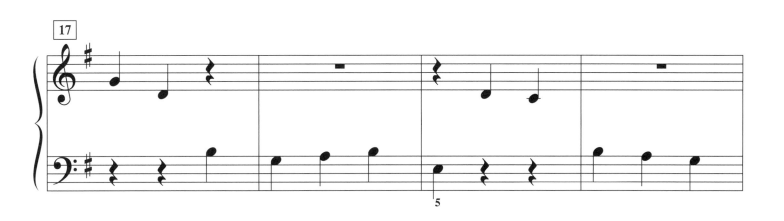

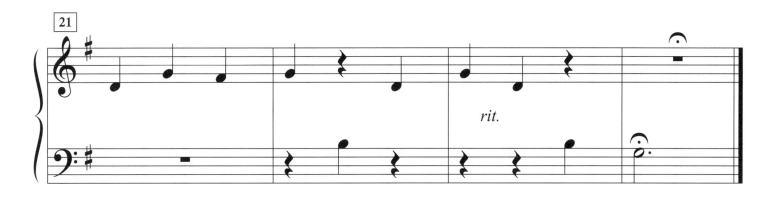

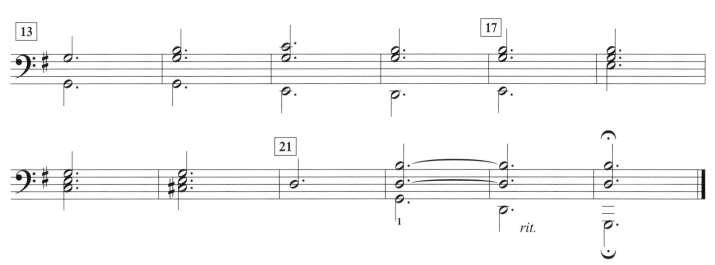

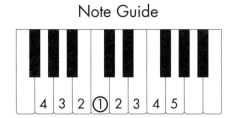

Note Guide

School Days

Music by Gus Edwards
Lyrics by Will Cobb

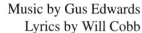

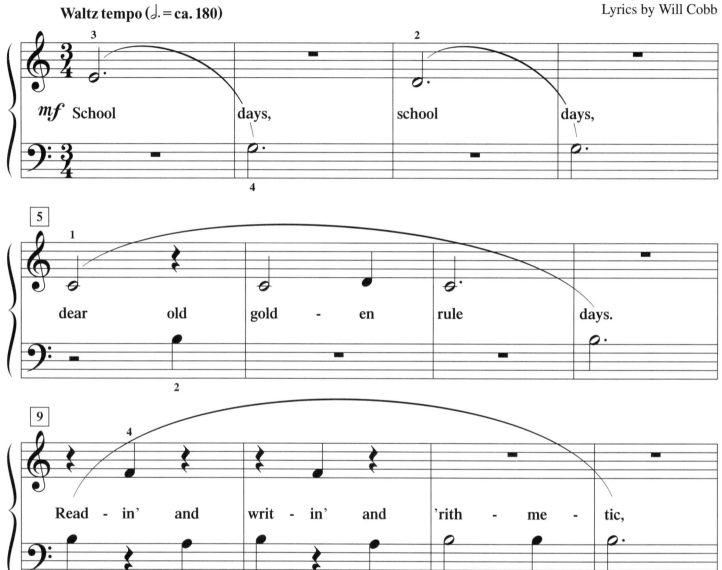

Teacher Duet: Student plays one octave higher.

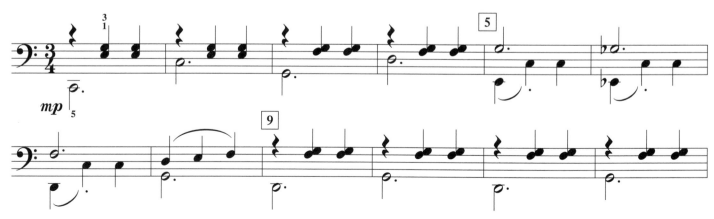

FJH2124

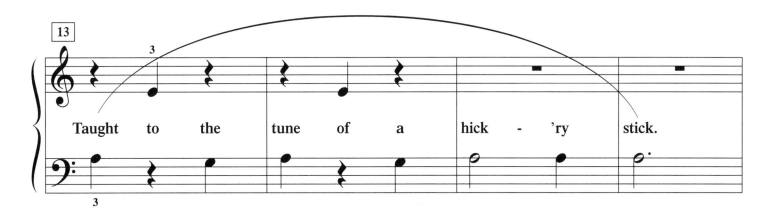

Taught to the tune of a hick - 'ry stick.

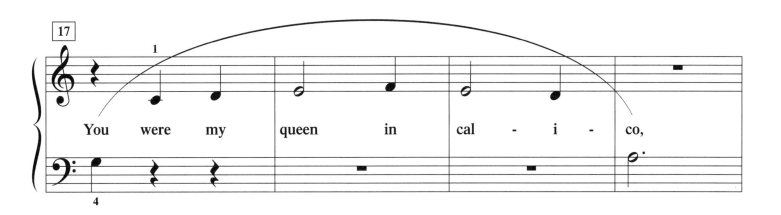

You were my queen in cal - i - co,

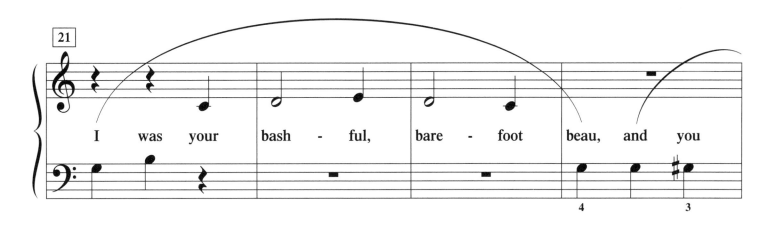

I was your bash - ful, bare - foot beau, and you

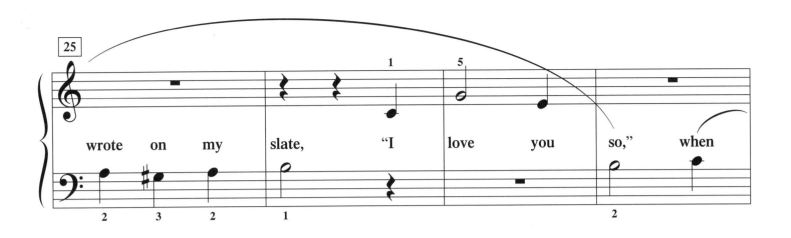

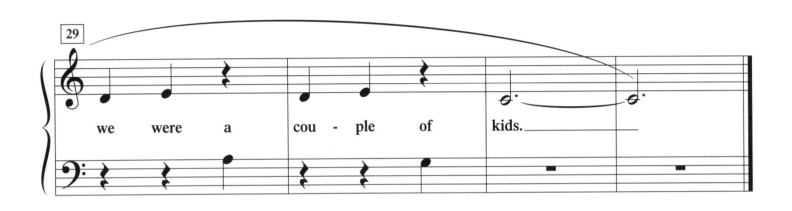

Note Guide

Aura Lee

Music by William Whiteman Fosdick
Lyrics by George R. Poulton

Gently (♩ = ca. 120)

mp As the black - bird in the spring 'neath the wil - low tree

Sat and piped I heard him sing, sing of Au - ra Lee.

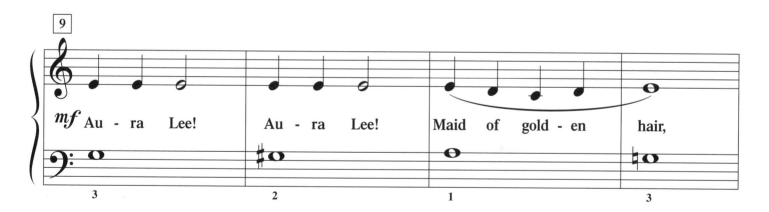

mf Au - ra Lee! Au - ra Lee! Maid of gold - en hair,

Teacher Duet: Student plays one octave higher.

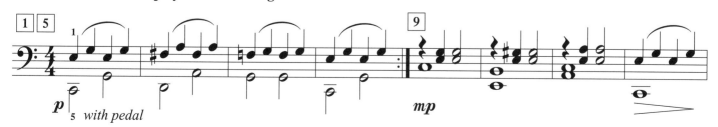

p 5 *with pedal* *mp*

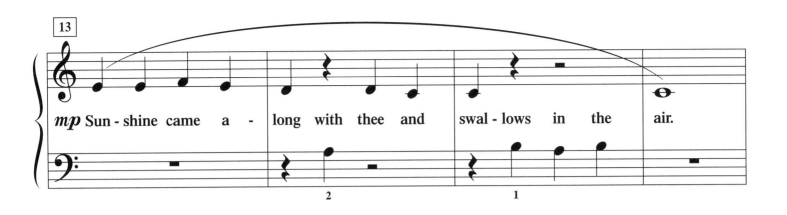

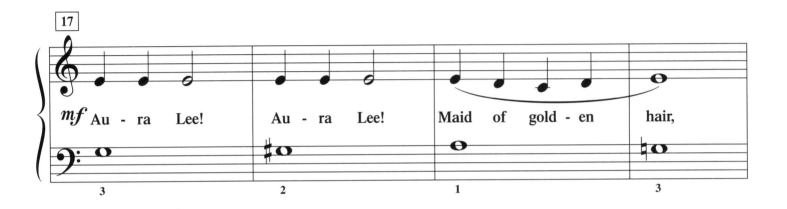

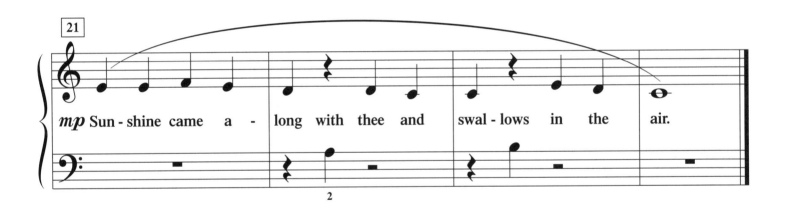

FJH2124

Note Guide

The Birthday Song

Patty Hill and Mildred Hill

Happily

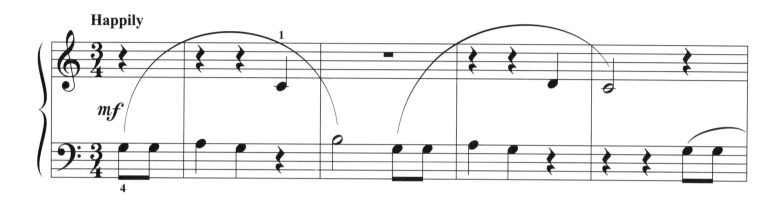

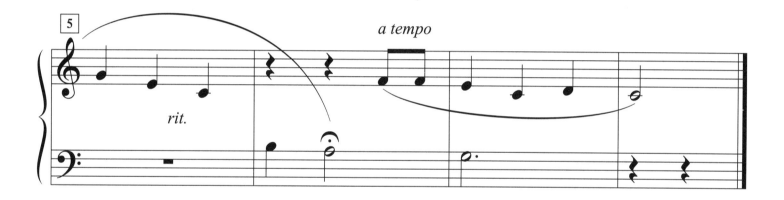

Teacher Duet: Student plays one octave higher.

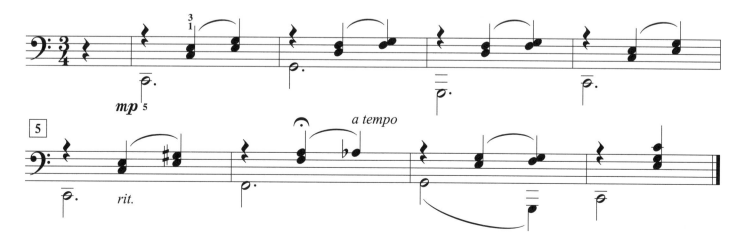

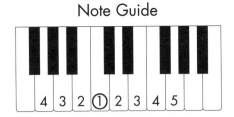

Note Guide

The Eensy Weensy Spider

Traditional

Allegretto (♩ = ca. 92)

mf The een - sy ween - sy spi - der climbed up the wa - ter - spout;

Down came the rain and washed the spi - der out.

Teacher Duet: Student plays one octave higher.

mp

FJH2124

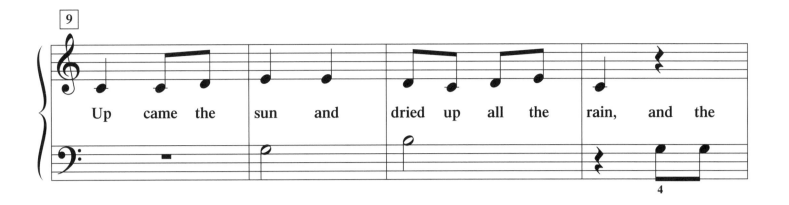

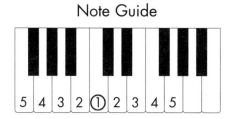

Home on the Range

Traditional

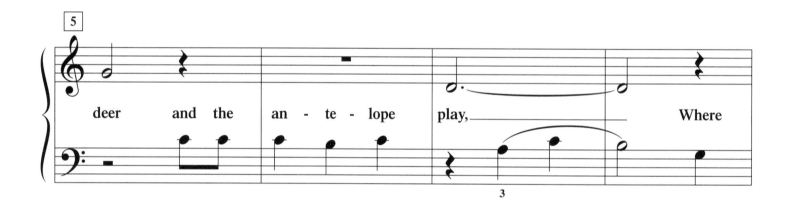

Teacher Duet: Student plays one octave higher.

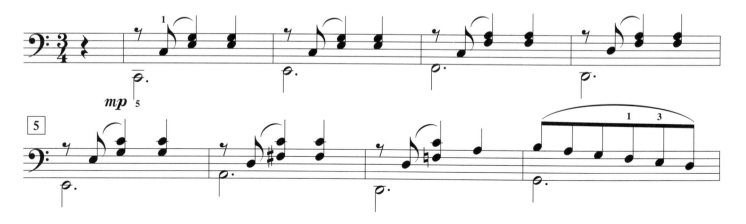

FJH2124

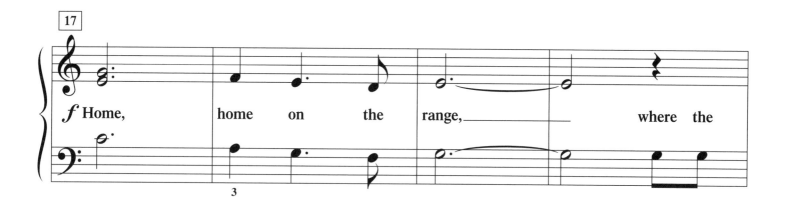

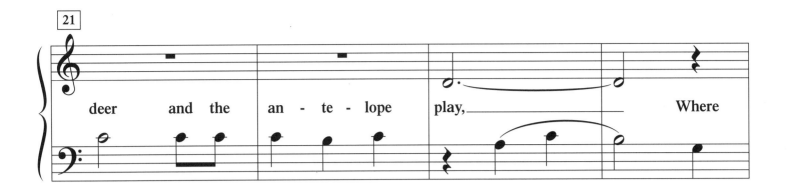

deer   and the   an - te - lope   play,_____   Where

sel - dom   is   heard   a   dis - cour - ag - ing   word,   And the

skies   are not   cloud - y   all   day._____

FJH2124

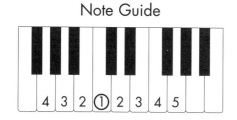

Note Guide

This Land Is Your Land

Woody Guthrie

Moderately fast (♩ = ca. 120)

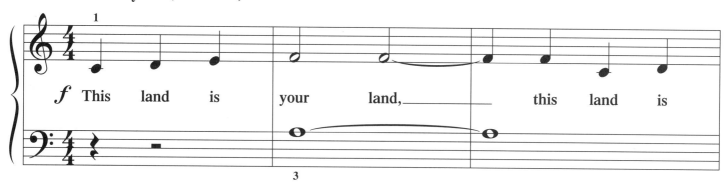

This land is your land,_____ this land is

my land_____ from Cal - i - for - nia_____

Teacher Duet: Student plays one octave higher.

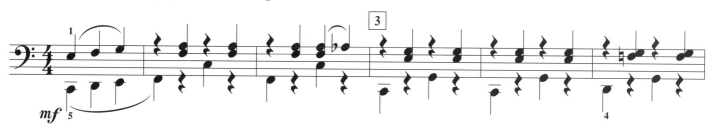

FJH2124

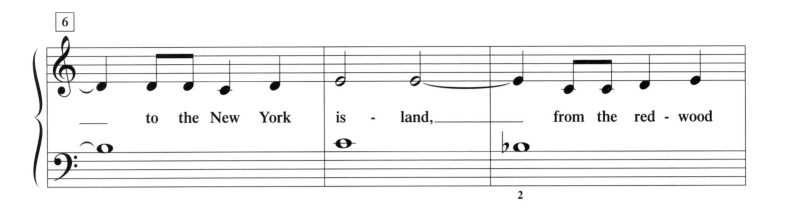

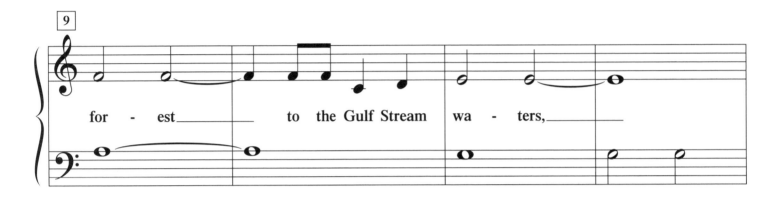

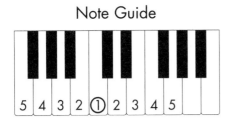

Note Guide

You're a Grand Old Flag

George M. Cohan

With spirit (♩ = ca. 100)

You're a grand old flag, you're a high-fly-ing flag, and for-

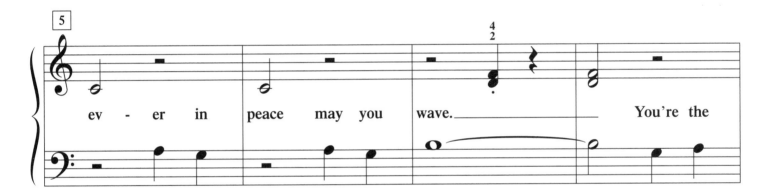

ev-er in peace may you wave._____ You're the

Teacher Duet: Student plays one octave higher.

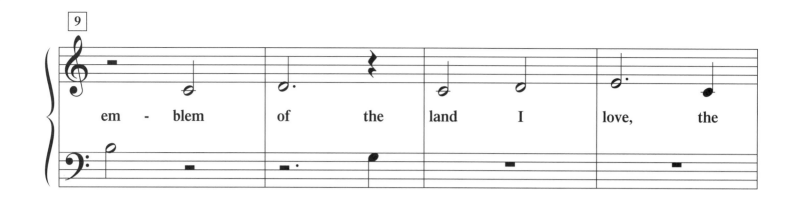

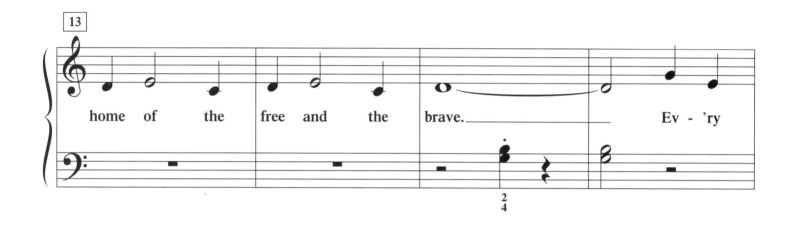

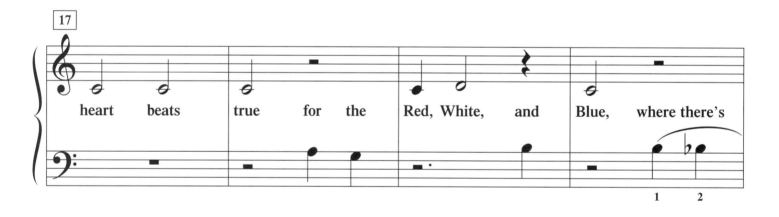

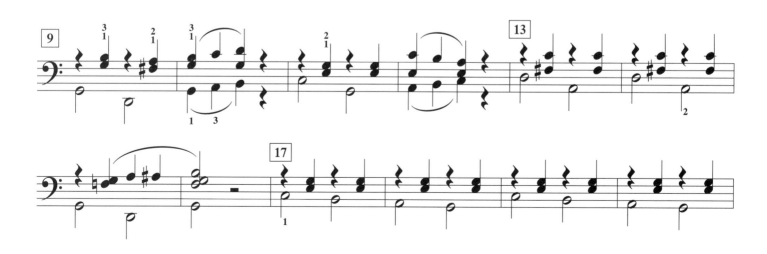

FJH2124

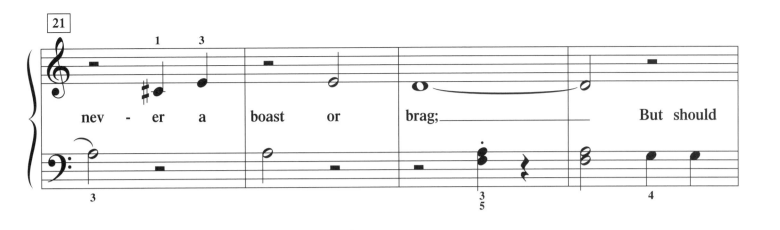

nev - er a boast or brag;_____ But should

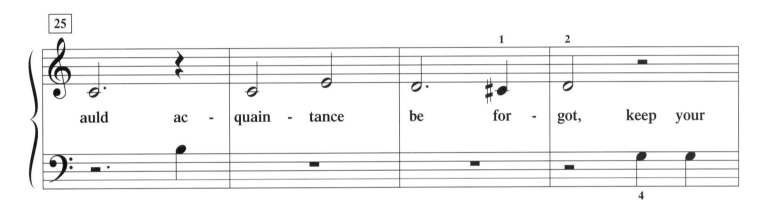

auld ac - quain - tance be for - got, keep your

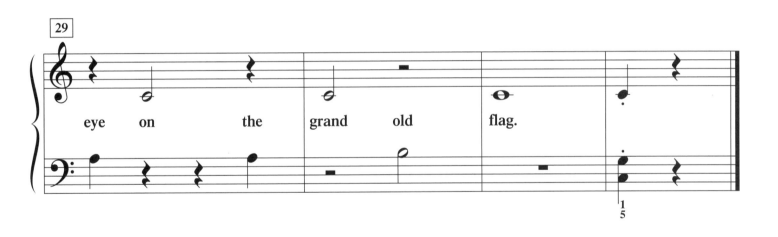

eye on the grand old flag.

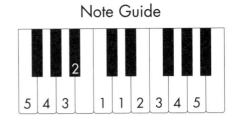

Note Guide

America, the Beautiful

Music by Samuel A. Ward
Lyrics by Katherine Lee Bates

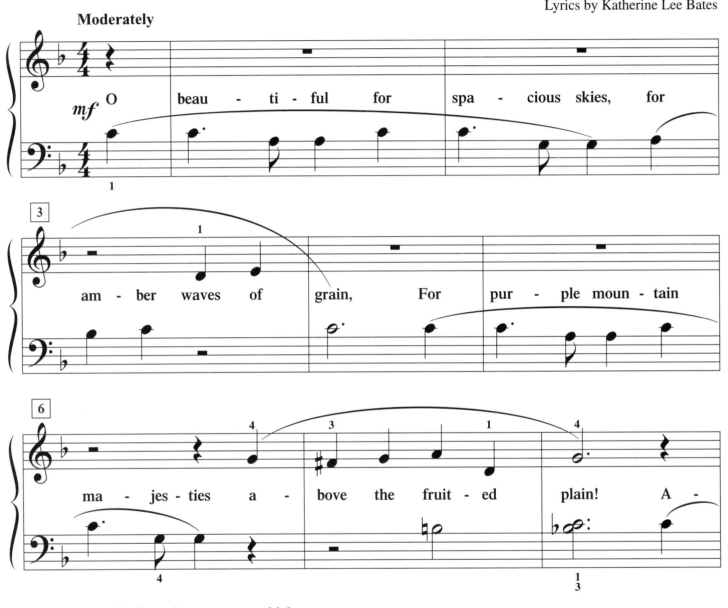

Moderately

mf O beau - ti - ful for spa - cious skies, for

am - ber waves of grain, For pur - ple moun - tain

ma - jes - ties a - bove the fruit - ed plain! A -

Teacher Duet: Student plays one octave higher.

mp *with pedal*

     FJH2124

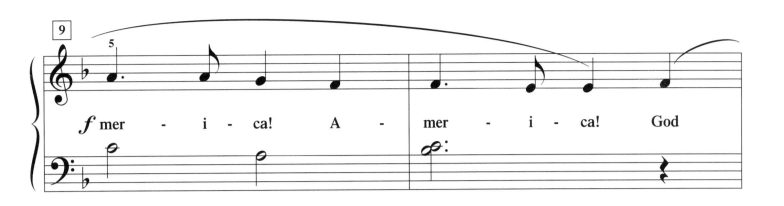

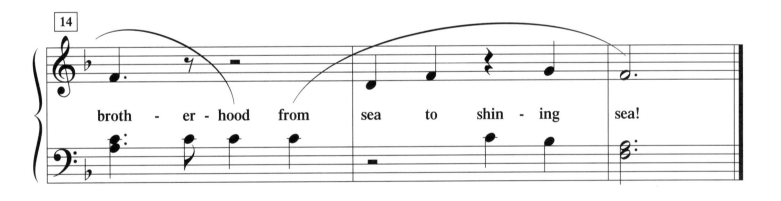
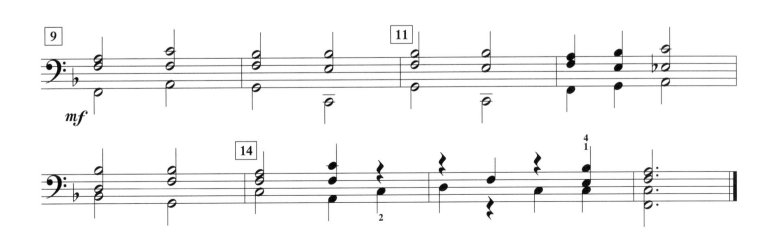

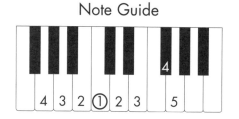

Note Guide

Marine's Hymn

Traditional

March tempo (♩ = ca. 120)

From the / Halls of / Mon - te - zu - / ma, to the
fight our / coun - try's bat - / tles in the

shores of / Tri - po - / **1.** li, / We
air, on / land, and

2. sea. / First to / fight for / right and

Teacher Duet: Student plays one octave higher.

mp

1. **2.**

FJH2124

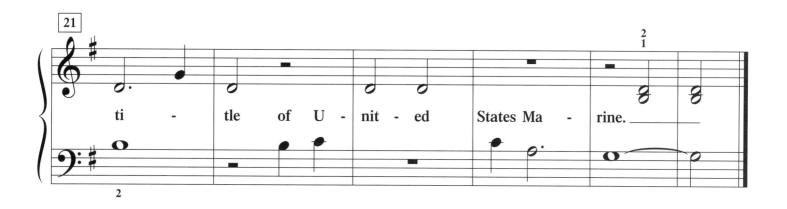

Note Guide

My Country, 'Tis of Thee
(America)

Samuel F. Smith

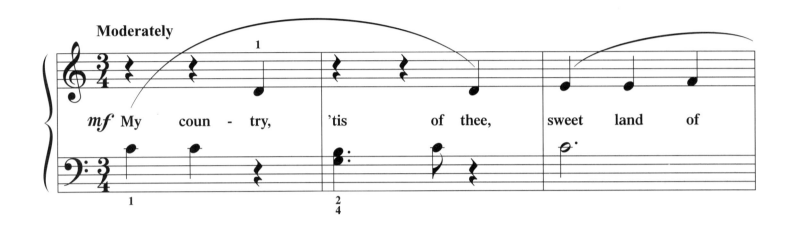

Moderately

mf My coun - try, 'tis of thee, sweet land of

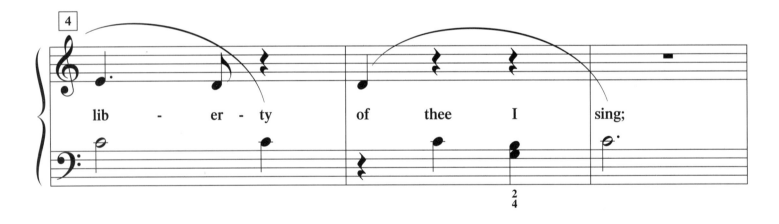

lib - er - ty of thee I sing;

Teacher Duet: Student plays one octave higher.

mp with pedal

FJH2124

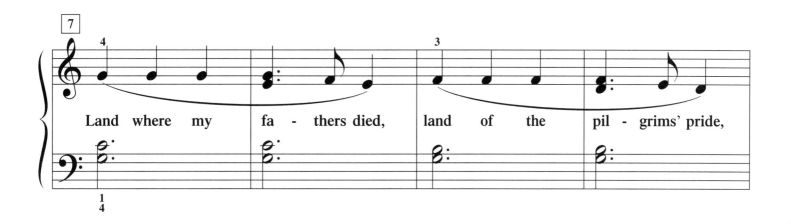

Land where my fa - thers died, land of the pil - grims' pride,

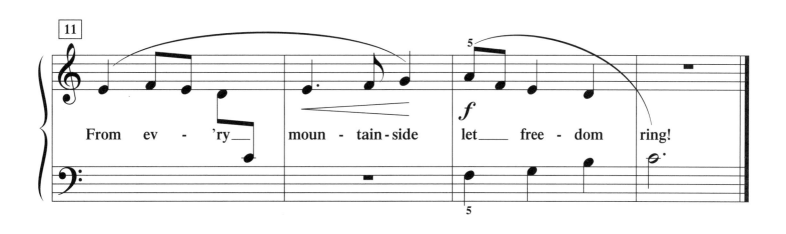

From ev - 'ry moun - tain-side let___ free - dom ring!

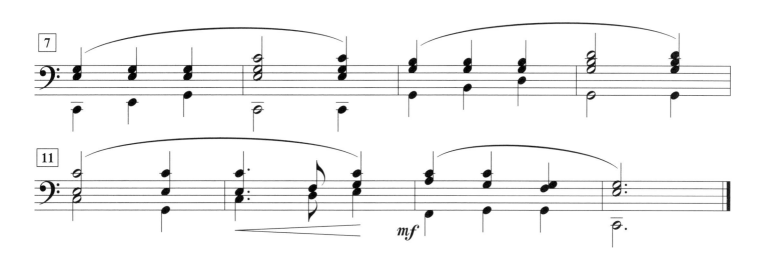

Note Guide

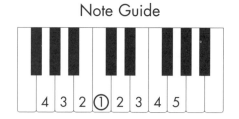

For the Beauty of the Earth

Music by Conrad Kocher
Lyrics by Folliott S. Pierpont

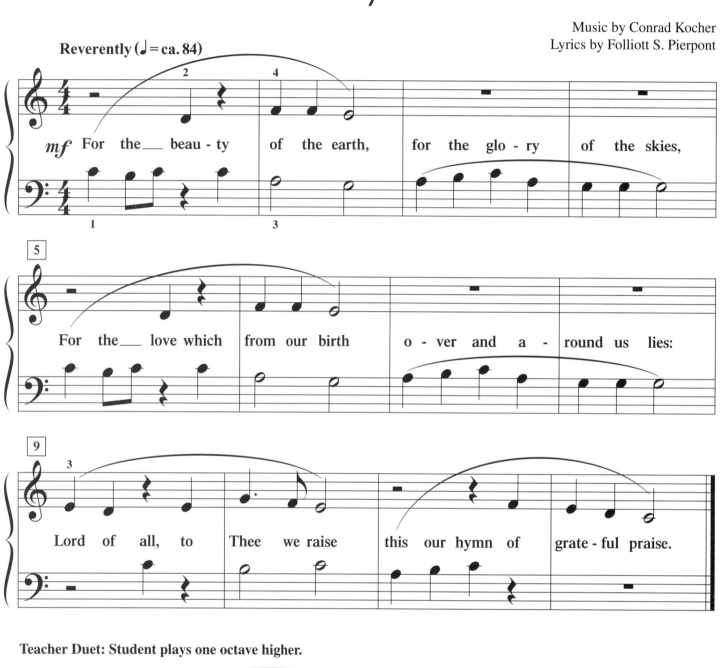

Reverently (♩ = ca. 84)

mf For the beau-ty of the earth, for the glo-ry of the skies,

For the love which from our birth o-ver and a-round us lies:

Lord of all, to Thee we raise this our hymn of grate-ful praise.

Teacher Duet: Student plays one octave higher.

mp

FJH2124

Note Guide

Amazing Grace

Music from *Virginia Harmony*
Lyrics by John Newton

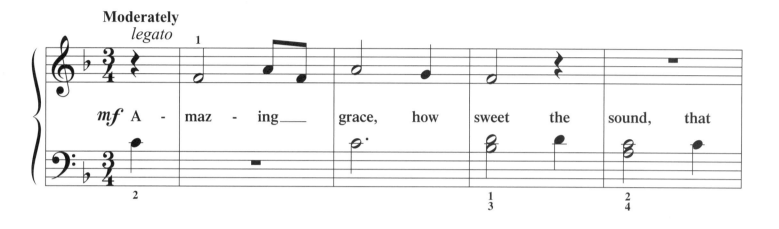

Moderately
legato

mf A - maz - ing___ grace, how sweet the sound, that

saved a___ wretch like___ me.___ I

Teacher Duet: Student plays one octave higher.

mp with pedal

FJH2124

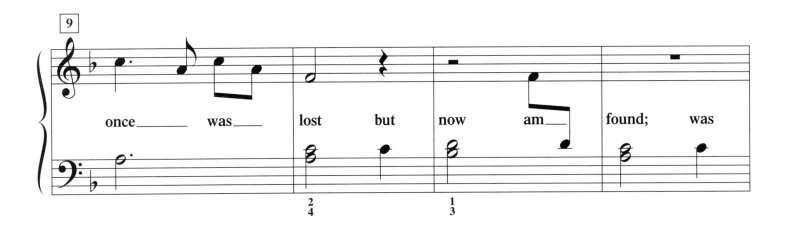

once_____ was_____ lost but now am_____ found; was

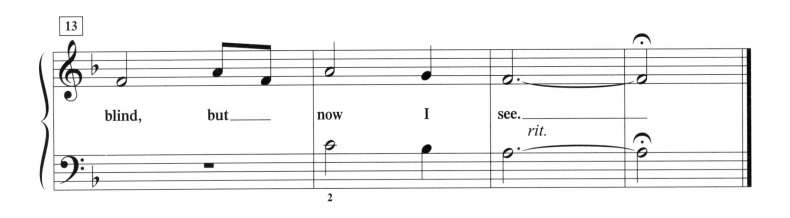

blind, but_____ now I see._____

rit.

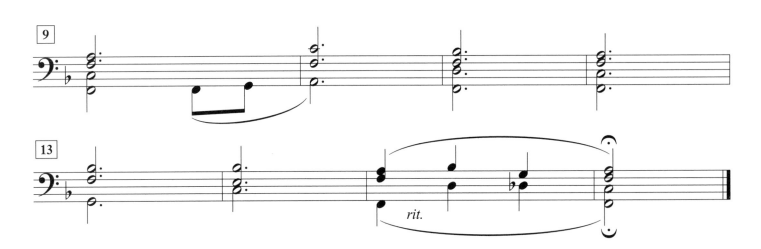

rit.

FJH2124

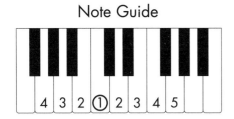

I'll Be a Sunbeam

Music by Edwin Excell
Lyrics by Nellie Talbot

Waltz tempo (♩. = ca. 60)

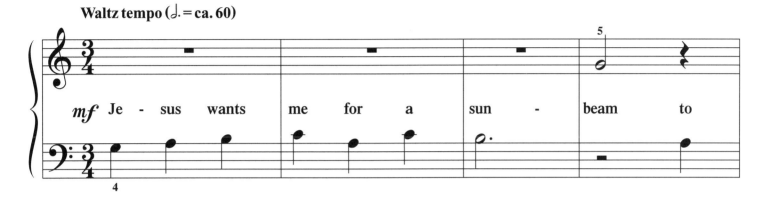

mf Je - sus wants me for a sun - beam to

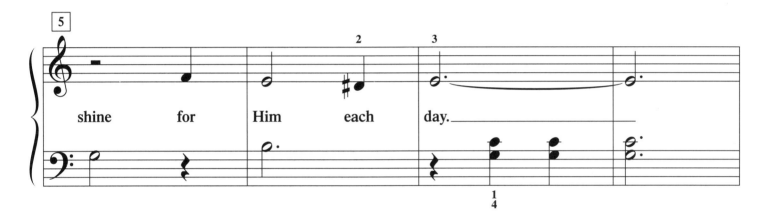

shine for Him each day.

Teacher Duet: Student plays one octave higher.

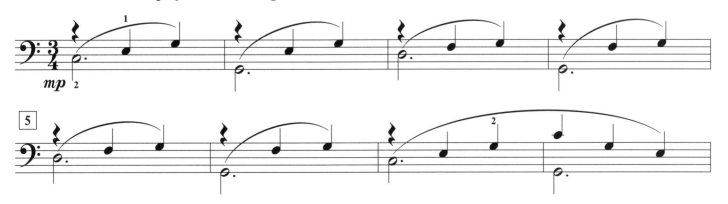

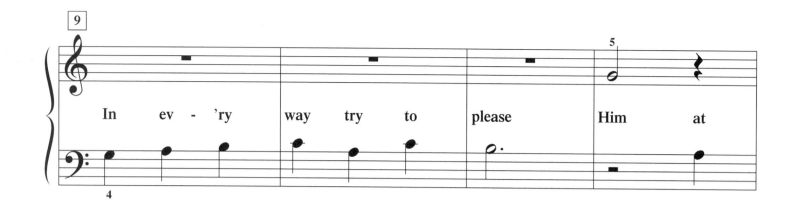

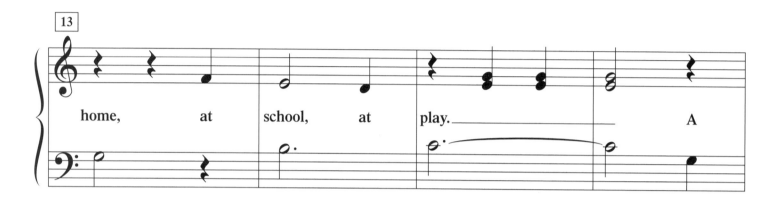

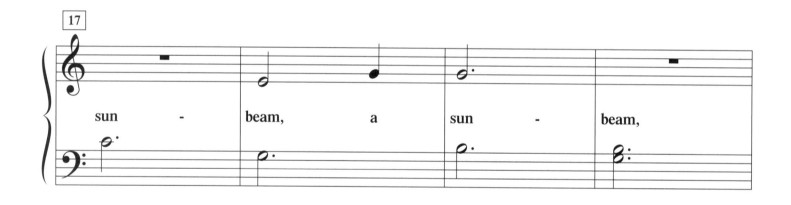

FJH2124

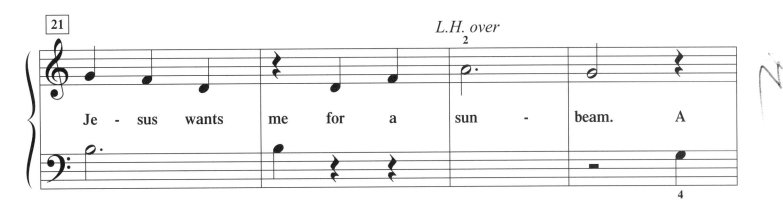

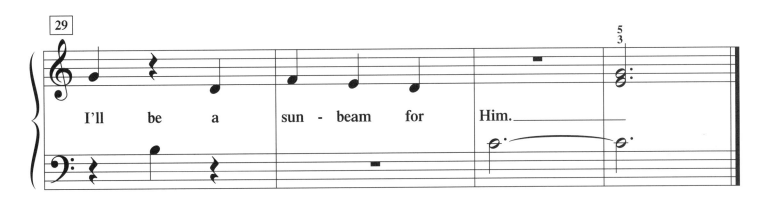

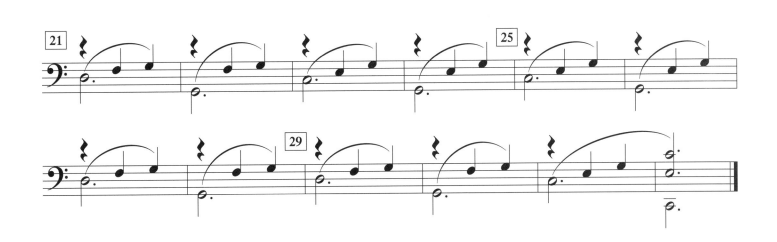

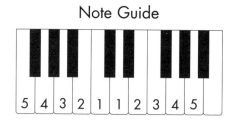

Note Guide

Nearer, My God, to Thee

Music by Lowell Mason
Lyrics by Sarah F. Adams

Slowly (♩ = ca. 80)

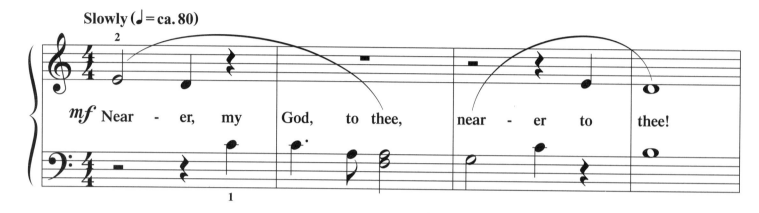

mf Near - er, my God, to thee, near - er to thee!

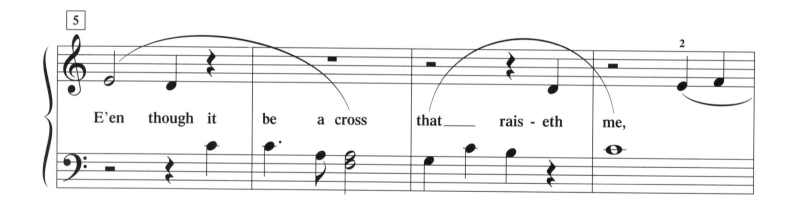

E'en though it be a cross that___ rais - eth me,

Teacher Duet: Student plays one octave higher.

mp
with pedal

FJH2124

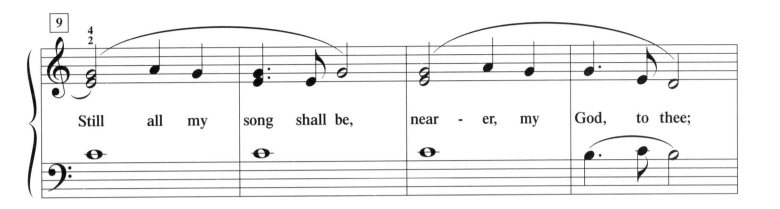

Still all my song shall be, near - er, my God, to thee;

Near - er, my God, to thee, near - er to thee! *p*

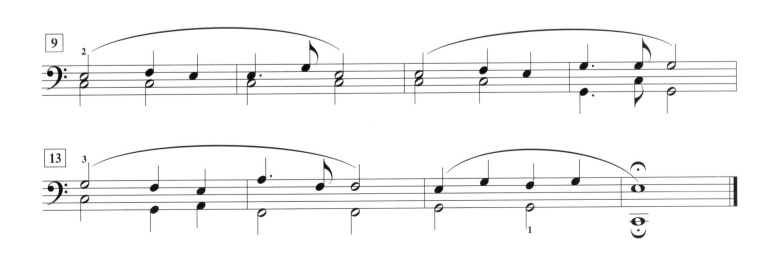

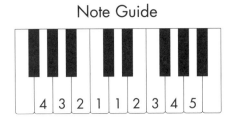

Note Guide

Swing Low, Sweet Chariot

African-American Spiritual

With a slow swing

mf Swing low, sweet char - i - ot,___ com-in' for to car-ry me

home; Swing___ low, sweet char - i - ot,___

Teacher Duet: Student plays one octave higher.

mp   *with pedal*

FJH2124

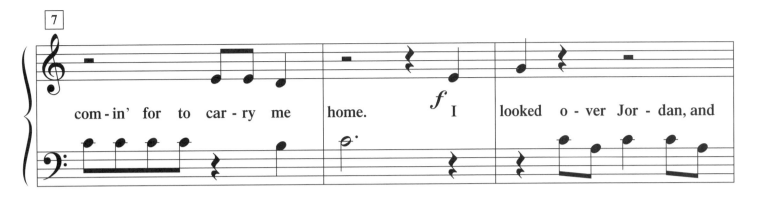

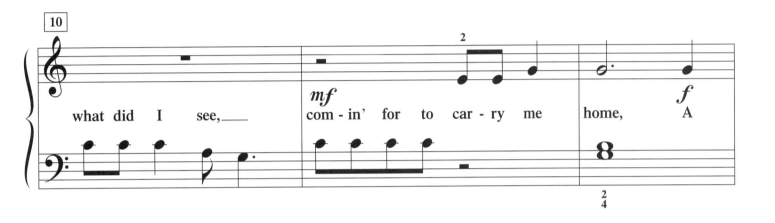

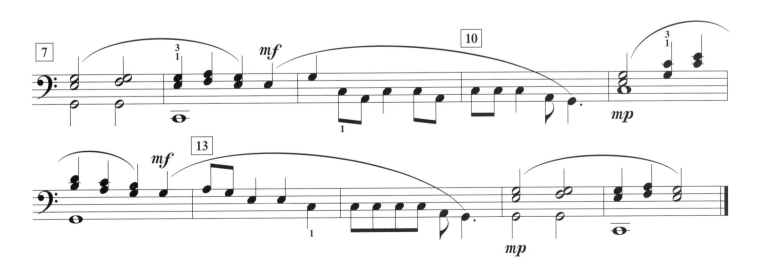

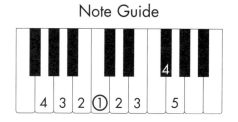

Note Guide

I Am a Child of God

Music by Mildred T. Pettit
Lyrics by Naomi Randall

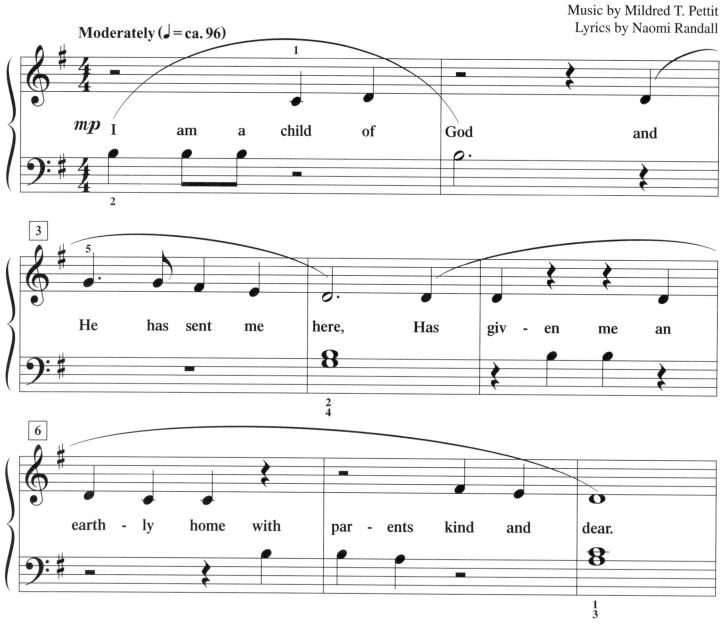

Moderately (♩ = ca. 96)

mp I am a child of God and He has sent me here, Has giv-en me an earth - ly home with par - ents kind and dear.

Teacher Duet: Student plays one octave higher.

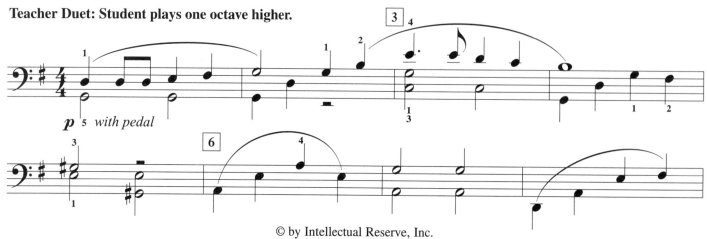

p with pedal

FJH2124

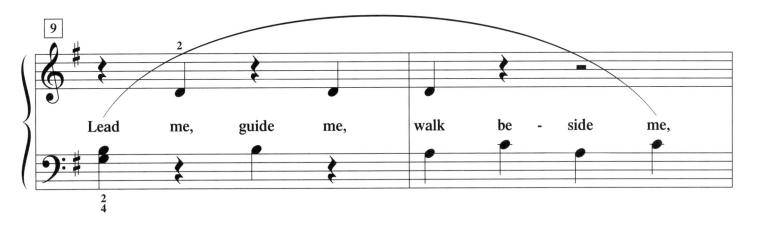

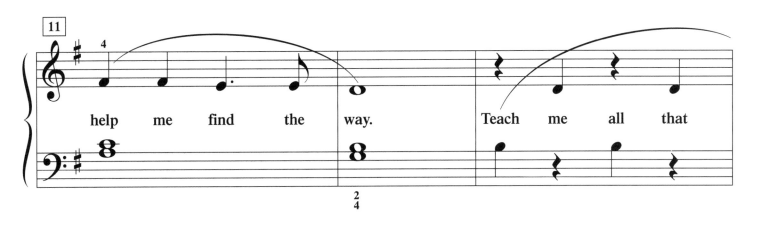

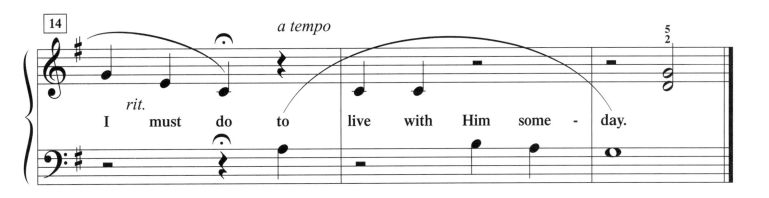

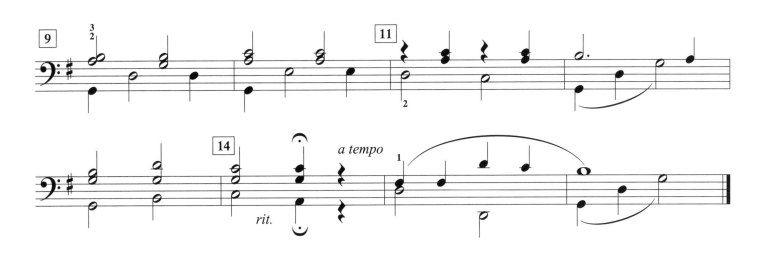

Note Guide

Jingle Bells

James Pierpont

Lively (♩ = ca. 100)

mf Dash - ing through the snow in a one - horse o - pen sleigh,

O'er the fields we go, laugh - ing all the way.

Teacher Duet: Student plays one octave higher.

mp

FJH2124

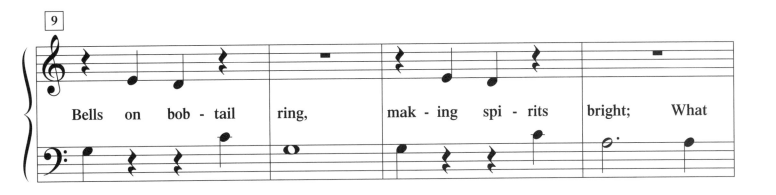

Bells on bob - tail ring, mak - ing spi - rits bright; What

fun it is to laugh and sing a sleigh-ing song to - night! Oh,

f jin - gle bells, jin - gle bells, jin - gle all the way.

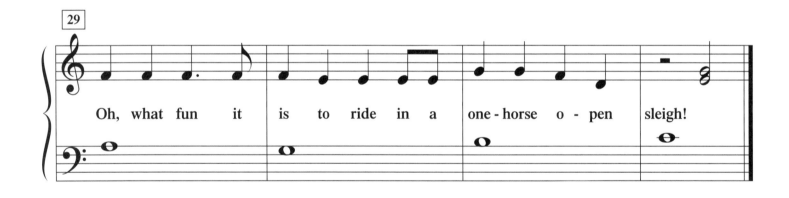

FJH2124

Note Guide

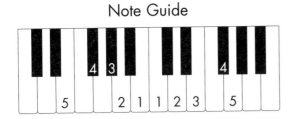

What Child Is This
(Greensleeves)

Music: English Folk Song
Lyrics by William Chatterton Dix

Andante

mp What child is this,___ who, laid to rest___ On

Ma - ry's lap___ is sleep - ing? Whom

Teacher Duet: Student plays one octave higher.

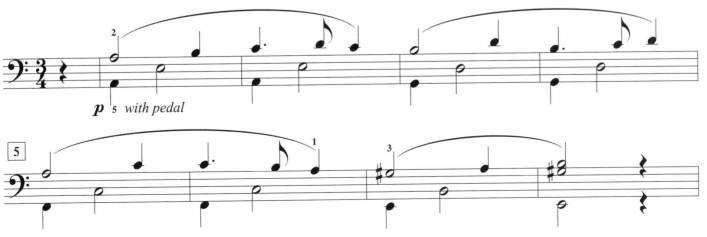

p 5 *with pedal*

FJH2124

an - gels   greet_____ with   an - thems   sweet_____ While

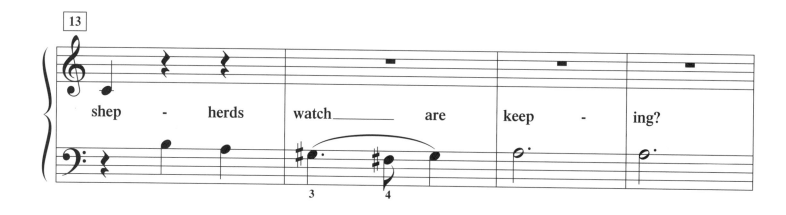

shep - herds   watch_____ are   keep - ing?

mf This,   this_____ is   Christ   the   king,_____ Whom

FJH2124

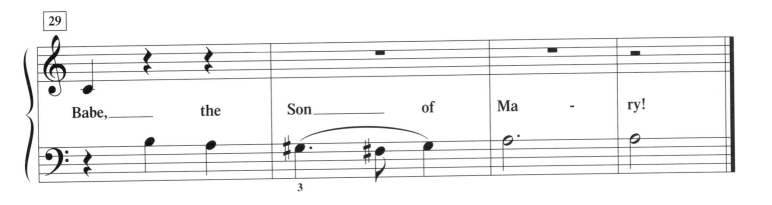

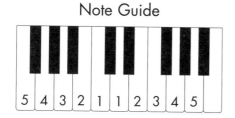

Note Guide

Up On the Housetop

Benjamin Hanby

Happily

mf Up on the house - top, rein - deer pause, out jumps good ol'

San - ta Claus! Down through the chim - ney with lots of toys,

all for the lit - tle ones, Christ - mas joys.

Teacher Duet: Student plays one octave higher.

mp

FJH2124

Note Guide

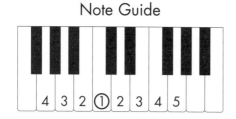

Oh Come, All Ye Faithful

(Adeste Fideles)

Music and lyrics by John F. Wade
Lyrics translated by Frederick Oakeley

Joyfully

mf Oh, come, all ye faith - ful,

Joy - ful and tri - um - phant! Oh, come ye, oh,

come _____ ye to Beth - le - hem;

Teacher Duet: Student plays one octave higher.

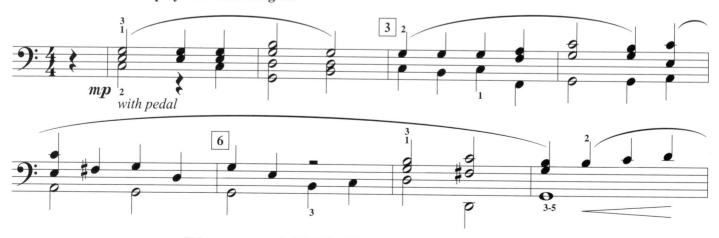

mp
with pedal

FJH2124

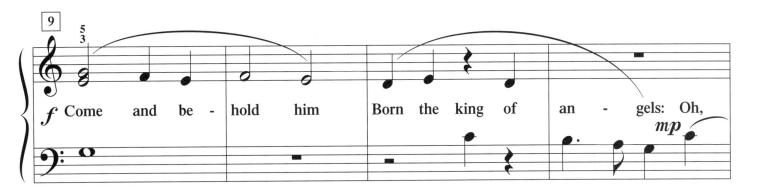

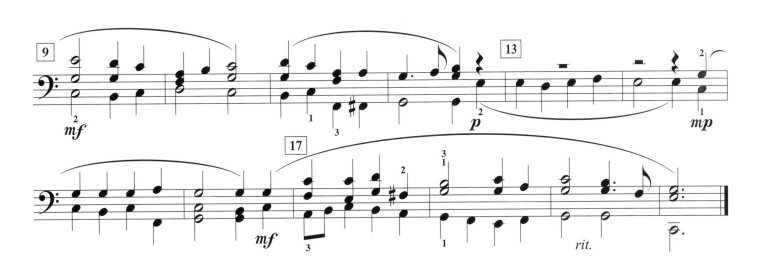

Note Guide

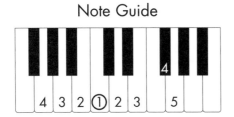

The First Noël

Traditional English Carol

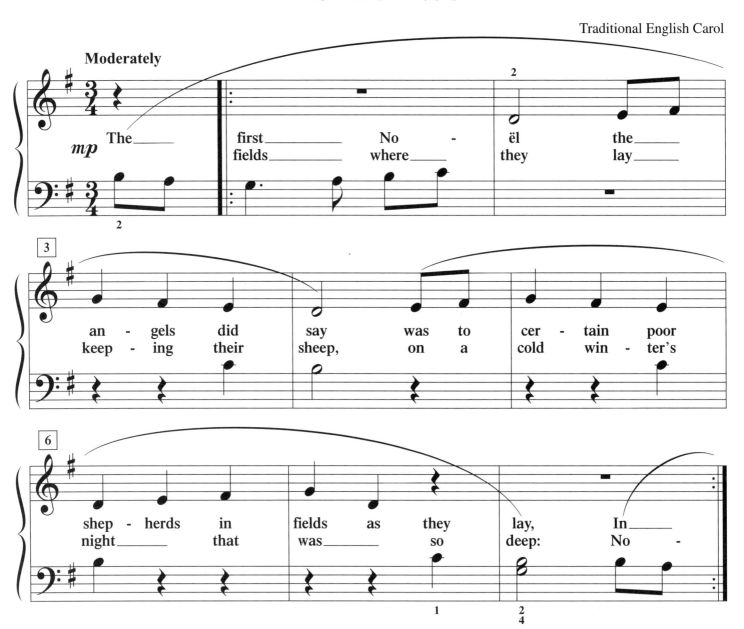

Teacher Duet: Student plays one octave higher.

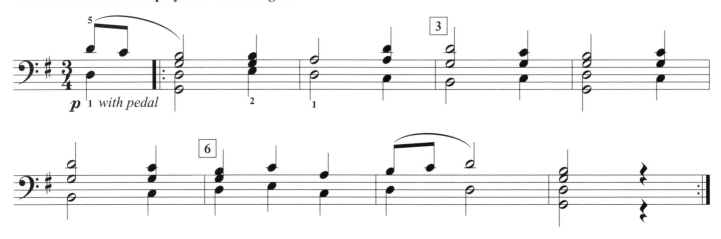

FJH2124

ël,_____ No - ël, No - ël, No - ël,

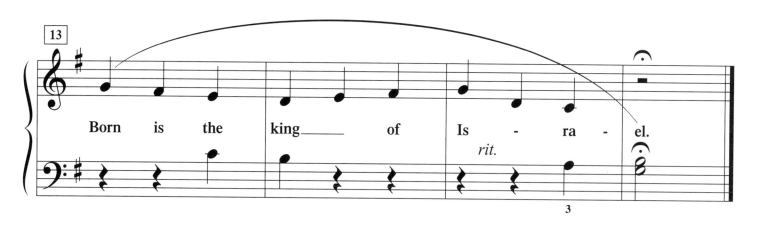

Born is the king_____ of Is - ra - el.

rit.

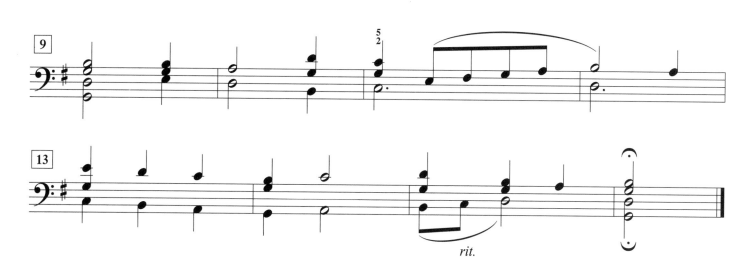